A Cool Little Book of Metaphysics

An Introduction to Psychic Ability and Energy Work

Books by Catherine Kane

Foresight Publications practical metaphysics

Adventures in Palmistry

The Practical Empath- Surviving and Thriving as a Psychic Empath

Manifesting Something Better: Easy, Quick and Fun Ways to Manifest the Life of Your Dreams

The Psychic Power of Your Dreams: Practical Skills for Working with Your Dreams for Insight, Information, Creativity and a Better Life

Magick for Pennies: Affordable Metaphysics for Everyone

Living in Interesting Times: Practical Energy Work When Times Get Tough

A Cool Little Book of Metaphysics: An Introduction to Psychic Ability and Energy Work

The Morgan and Sam urban fantasy series

The Lands That Lie Between

The Swans of War

The Song of Dreams and Shadows

A Cool Little Book of Metaphysics

An Introduction to Psychic Ability and Energy Work

By Catherine Kane

Foresight Publications
Wallingford, Ct.

A Cool Little Book of Metaphysics-An Introduction to Psychic Ability and Energy Work © June 2022
By Catherine Kane

All Rights Reserved.

No parts of this book may be reproduced or transmitted in any form, or by any means, electronic or mechanical, including photocopying, recording or by any information storage or retrieval system, without written permission from the author, except for brief quotations in a review.

ISBN: 978-0-9846951-8-8

Foresight Publications
Wallingford, CT.

Table of Contents

Introduction 1
Free Will 2
How Readings Can Be Useful 3
Different Kinds of Readings 5
Are You Psychic? 8
Tapping into Your Psychic Ability- Pendulum 9
Tapping into Your Psychic Ability- Listen to Your Body 12
Energy 14
The Law of Attraction 15
Setting an Intention 17
Clearing Negative Energy 18
Energetic Shielding 20
Focus 22
Affirmations 24
More Things to Learn 26

Introduction

The world is a magical place, full of magical energy, and psychic abilities let us interact with that energy and do things with it.

Unfortunately, modern society as a whole doesn't accept that. It's uncomfortable with it and tends to shunt magic, energy work and psychic abilities into the category of movies and fairy tales. It has few supports for folks who are energetically active or psychically aware

And that's a bit of a problem, because not everyone has access to metaphysical teachers or mentors. Not everyone receives an invitation to a magical school or has a wise and knowledgeable magical mentor turn up on their doorstep. Not everyone knows that these abilities are real, let alone how to learn them.

And that's where this booklet comes in.

Hi. I'm Catherine Kane. I'm a professional psychic, a Reiki master, a New Age chick, a teacher of practical magic and alternative medical techniques, an author and an enthusiastic student of the universe, and I've been exploring the unseen universe for over 50 years. I like to help people and to empower them to find and live their best and brightest dreams.

This booklet will not tell you everything about the world of metaphysics. It will however give you some basic practical information about energy, free will, psychic ability, protecting yourself and other helpful topics to get you started; and it'll point you in some useful directions if you decide to go further.

The journey of a thousand miles begins with a single step. So, let's get started.

__Free Will__

Let's start at the beginning.

You have free will. God, Goddess, the Universe or whoever you believe in has given you the ability to make choices, good, bad or indifferent, and by making choices, have a certain amount of control over your life. Not total control, but some.

And that means that the future's not fixed, because, at any time, you can choose to change the direction in life that you're going and head off in a new direction.

And when you do that, your future changes. The cards can change, as can the lines in your palm…

Given that, you might question how anyone can do an accurate reading for you. That's ok, we're going to get into that in the next chapter.

Before we go there though, it's really important to emphasize that you are in charge of your own life and your own future. You are the captain of your own ship.

You're not the only person who can affect your life, of course. Other people's actions can affect you as well. Some of them you can control and some of them you can't, and it's important to be able to tell the difference.

And it's important to know that, in life, there is no "doom"/ there is no "fate". There are only choices. Your choices.

If you find yourself feeling overwhelmed, like you have no options, stop, take a deep breath, remind yourself that you have free will, look at your options and then you choose.

Free Will rocks that way.

How Readings Can Be Useful

In the last chapter, we talked about free will, and how you have the ability to change the direction of your life if you choose to

This raises the question of, if you can change the direction of your life and therefore change your future, how can anyone actually do an accurate psychic reading for you?

The answer is pretty simple. A reading done by a knowledgeable, ethical and accurate reader can show your future- but it only shows the future you're heading into if you keep doing what you're doing. You're still free to change the direction of your life and, if you do, the future can change and a new reading will reflect that new future.

(It's worth noting that people are not surprised if you get new cards in a tarot reading, but don't realize that the lines in your palm can change if you change your life enough. Indeed, I've seen palms change **while I read them** if information from the original reading made a big enough impression.)

From my experience, this is one of the best reasons I can think of to get a reading- to get a headsup whether my life is heading towards a future I'll like, or whether I need to make what I call a "course correction" to avoid something I don't want. (There are other good reasons to get a reading but this one tops my list.)

At that point, I usually try to start my readings with a quick lecture on the nature of free will. How, if you get a reading you don't like, you can usually change that by just changing the direction in which your life is headed. How you're not just stuck with what the reading said.

There is no "doom". There is no "fate".

There are only choices.

I believe that too many people assign too much power to readers and what we tell them. Turn their lives over to the reading when they don't have to.

I look upon readings as a helpful reference, a second opinion so you can make better choices. I'm here to put you in the driver's seat, not take over your life.

And when a person being read understands how free will and readings work, this means they're in a better space to get the best use out of the reading.

We look at ourselves as the traffic guys on the road of life- we're here to tell you where the jams are so you can "take alternate route."

Different Kinds of Readings

Folks ask "What's the best type of psychic reading?"

The answer is "They all are!" In the hands of a knowledgeable and ethical reader, any modality can give you a useful reading. They all have individual strengths and weaknesses, but, at the end of the day, a psychic modality is just a way to let the reader get in touch with her inner wisdom.

That being said, here's some information on some modalities.

- Palmistry- Covers the person's entire life. Defines strengths and weaknesses. If the client changes the direction of their life, their lines change to reflect the new future or past. Is all about the person whose hand is being read. Other people only appear in regards to how they affect that person.
- Tarot- Requires equipment. More people familiar with it. Can do a general reading or address a specific topic. Sometimes a client sees something in the images on the cards which speaks to them, even if it doesn't relate to the traditional meaning of the cards. (That should be paid attention to as it's often a message from Spirit.) Reading can get garbled if person being read has a lot of questions- at that point, it's better to do multiple readings, chose a different modality or do a general reading (with the understanding that the general reading may give the info the universe feels the person needs as opposed to what they want.) Lots of research material out there, but some sources are clearer to a student than others, so choose carefully.

- Runes- Requires equipment. Less people are familiar with it, which can make it feel either less desirable or more exotic. Good at showing outside influences on client, and the interplay between them. Otherwise, similar to the pros and cons for tarot.
- I Ching- Requires equipment. Requires a specific question or issue to be read for. Very focused. Most readers do not speak Chinese and will work from a translation. Some translations are more obscure than others, which can mask the message, so a user-friendly translation is helpful.
- Oracle cards- Some people discount them as fluffy or light weight. My experience has been that there's a wide variety of oracle cards out there and the right deck (one that you connect with as reader or person being read) can give as powerful a reading as any other modality. Requires equipment. Like tarot, sometimes a client sees something in the images that has nothing to do with the standard meaning but that speaks to them. (This can be also be a direct message from Spirit, and should be treated with respect.) Some people will look down on oracle cards. More flexible than some other modalities.
- Pendulum dowsing- Requires equipment. Answers "yes/ no" questions. For that reason, limited for doing readings, but great if what you need is a clear "yes/no".

The bottom line is that they're all good.

The main key to a good reading is not the modality. It's being able to ask a good question- one that's clear, is specific enough to get a clear answer, limits variables and that's open to getting an answer that's not necessarily the one you want.

If you're having problems getting a clear answer in your reading, it may be that the problem is your question- it may

- Have too many variables.
- Be too ambiguous. ("will this job be good for me?" as opposed to "will I be happy in this job?")
- Be leading.

At that point, you may need to rephrase it or narrow the question's focus, so that Spirit can give you a clearer answer.

And it's worth keeping in mind the factor of Free Will, that the answer only indicates the direction your life is headed and that you can change that direction.

Any modality is a structure for bringing your inner wisdom through, whether you're getting a reading or doing one. Listen to your inner voice, choose the modality that speaks to you, practice it and trust your intuition.

Are You Psychic?

I don't know if everyone is psychic (I haven't met everyone yet.) but, in my lifetime, a majority of the folks I've encountered seem to have some degree of psychic ability, whether active or latent. Most people have some kind of instincts, or intuition, or "hunches" or other names for knowing things without knowing how they know them.

Have you ever:

- Thought of someone you haven't been in contact with for awhile and then gotten a call from them?
- Started humming a tune just before it comes on on the radio?
- Taken a different route home from work because of a feeling, and later found out traffic was backed up on your usual route?

Those are all examples of unconscious psychic activity.

And you can learn how to use your psychic ability consciously. Build psychic muscle and skills.

Now there's lots of ways that you can build these skills. In the next two chapters, I'll be teaching you two simple ways to tap into your inner wisdom to get you started.

Tapping into Your Psychic Ability- Pendulum

There are lots of different ways to tap into your own psychic intuition. Meditation. Cards, whether oracle or tarot. Channeling. Energy work.

This is just a basic primer though, so I'm going to teach you two simple methods to get you started.

The first is using a pendulum.

A pendulum is a weighted item hanging from a chain, cord, ribbon or other flexible item it can swing freely from. Something to hold onto at the other end from the weight is helpful but optional.

You can buy one at a new age store or you can make one for yourself. My husband's first pendulum was a sinker on the end of a piece of fishing line. In a pinch, I've used a necklace.

Next, you experiment with holding the far end of the chain or cord in a way that lets the pendulum swing freely in all directions. I like to brace my elbow so the pendulum is more stable. Pick a method of holding it so that you're less likely to unconsciously affect the swing.

Next, you and your pendulum need to learn to communicate with each other.

I start by asking it "show me yes" (and because I was raised to be polite, "show me yes, please" is my go-to.) The pendulum will begin to swing. Note which way it swings as this is this pendulum's "yes" for you.

Repeat with "show me no please." It will show you it's no for you.

If the movements are tiny, try saying "bigger, please". Sometimes a pendulum needs encouragement to speak up.

For me, most pendulums go forwards and back for yes and side to side for no, but that's not true for everyone. A pendulum may also have one type of yes for one person and a different one for a different person. It's best to try it out for yourself.

The bigger the swing, the bigger the "yes" or the "no".

A third request is "stop, please" to get it to stop between answers for clarity.

And the final thing you may see is when the pendulum goes what I call "wonky". Alternates rapidly between yes and no. Goes in circles. Twitches and rocks in an irregular manner. Stops dead. This is usually an indicator that you've asked the question in a way that can't be answered either yes or no, and the poor pendulum doesn't know what to do with that. (Ex: "will this job I'm offered be good for me?" If it'll make you a lot of money but also drive you crazy, the pendulum is going to have a hard time coming up with an accurate yes or no. If the response is wonky, you might want ask "will I be happy with this job?" or "will the money be as good as they're saying at this job?")

Practice with your pendulum to get used to working with it. Once you're comfortable, start asking it questions that you know the answers to.

- Am I a woman?
- Is it raining now?

Once you've got comfortable with that, try questions you don't know the answers to but can check.

- Will it snow tonight?
- Will my family member be home by 5:30 pm?

And the final step, once you've passed step 2, is to ask yes/ no questions that you can't check.

Working with your pendulum over time will help you to build confidence over time so you can use it as a way to contact your own intuition.

A pendulum is a limited tool for divination but it's great at what it does, which is clear answers to "yes/no" questions. The key to getting the best results from a pendulum is learning how to ask good questions, and that's something you learn with time, so the best way to learn good pendulum skills is to practice, practice, practice.

Tapping into Your Psychic Ability- Listen to Your Body

The second method we'll discuss is listening to what your body has to tell you about things and people and circumstances.

Let's start with a baseline.

Close your eyes and think about something or someone you like. Take a minute (or even a few) and really get into this.

Now stop and take a mental snapshot. How do you feel when you do this? Where do you feel it?

Are you sitting up straighter? Are your muscles relaxed? Are you smiling?

This is your positive feeling. Your "yes".

Now close your eyes again and think of someone or something you don't like. Take a moment or two (I'm sorry) and sit with this.

Now stop and take another mental snapshot. How do you feel when you do this? Where do you feel it?

Do you have tension or pain? In your shoulders, your back, your head? Are you gritting your teeth? Do you feel drained?

This is your negative feeling. Your "no".

Go back and visit your yes again to balance yourself out.

This seems very simple, but it's one of the most useful techniques you can become familiar with because it requires no equipment and can be done almost anywhere to get in touch with your inner wisdom without looking odd or startling people. You can use it to ask your inner wisdom questions like

- Which book or class will help me more?
- Should I accept this invitation or not?
- Which movie will I enjoy more?
- Which menu offering will please me more?
- Should I go straight home from work or take "the scenic route"?

Your body is talking to you, and if you listen, it can help you make contact with your intuition.

This technique is part of a larger field referred to "energetic kinesiology".

Energy

Let's move from psychic ability to energy work.

The universe is made of energy. Magickal energy. The people and things that we believe are solid are actually made up of atoms, which are tiny particles connected by energy fields.

Every one of those energy fields is vibrating and every one of those vibrations can change, depending on things like the situation it's in and what other energy fields it's exposed to.

One of the ways that an energy field can change another is a process known as entrainment. When two energy fields are in contact, the less powerful one will gradually shift until it's in harmony with the stronger one (kinda like how, when a group of people are singing together, the singers will gradually shift to be in harmony with whoever is singing the loudest.) The more powerful field sets the level for the other fields around it.

For this reason, it's a good idea to keep your vibrations positive as a stronger higher vibration will tend to shift energy around you in a direction that will support your happiness.

An energy field also tends to attract other energy fields that vibrate at the same level as it does. This includes your own energy field. The higher the vibrational level of your energy field, the more likely you are to attract, people, things and activities that you'd prefer. The lower your level of vibration, the more likely to attract things you don't like.

We're going to talk about how this works and how to make it work for you more in the next chapter.

The Law of Attraction

In metaphysics, there are a number of laws or rules. These are actually definitions of how things work in the world of energy. One of the most important, as well as well known, is the Law of Attraction. This law basically says that what you give most of your attention to is what you're gonna get more of. (If you want to put it more elegantly, "Where attention goes, the energy flows.")

So basically, whatever you focus the majority of your attention is what you're gonna attract more of into your life – and also things that vibrate at the same energetic level.

- So, focus on chocolate chip cookies, attract more chocolate chip cookies- and also hot fudge sundaes.
- Focus on bills, attract more bills- and also tax hikes.

So why is that?

Evidently whatever you give a majority of your focus to will set your own energy field to the same vibrational level- which attracts more things that vibrate on a similar level. Which, if you're focusing primarily on things that you like, you'll attract more of those things, and if you're focusing on things you don't want, you'll attract more of that vibration.

It's not an absolute all-or-nothing thing, but, either way, it increases the chances of getting more of what you're sorting for. At that point, it makes sense to tip the odds in your favor, and keep your vibrational levels higher.

This doesn't mean ignoring things that you don't like or that are lower vibration, such as bills, corruption or cleaning out the cat box. Ignoring those would mean more problems piling up, and that won't boost positive vibrations. It means giving your challenges only as much attention as they require to deal with them, and no more so. It means dealing with those things as quickly and efficiently as possible before returning your focus to more positive things. It means giving more of your attention to things that make you feel good as opposed to those that make you feel bad.

And it doesn't mean you can't have a bad hair day or feel depressed. Everyone does. It just means that it's a good thing to do your best in any moment to accept being down or cranky, not beat yourself up over it, and return your focus to something more positive as soon as you can manage it (even if your positive is something small like kittens, or dandelions, or ice cream.)

Most vibrational shifts don't happen immediately. Most take a little while to actually shift and start attracting like energies, so if you have a down turn, there's usually time to turn your energy around.

Sometimes, though, you need to clean out negative energy or shield yourself from negative energy around you. We're going to get into that in a couple of chapters coming up.

But first, let's talk about setting an intention.

Setting an Intention

One of the basic parts of most metaphysical practices is intention.

- You raise or gather energy, by things such as physical activity, focusing on positive things, or other activities we've discussed in various parts of this booklet.
- You set an intention for what you want that energy to do.
- You use focus and will to send that energy to do it.

Intention is a fancy- schmancy way of saying "goal/objective". It's giving that energy a target or a purpose.

It's a good idea to clearly define what you want before you start energy work, so you don't wobble, go off track or otherwise change your intention in the middle of things.

There's a lot of ways of setting an intention. You can hold it in your mind as you work with energy. You can say it out loud. (ie "I bring more money into my life!") You can write it down. You can say or write it multiple times, a la affirmations.

The important thing is to focus clearly on what you're trying to do when you're doing it.

If you don't know where you're going, you're probably not going to get there.

We're gonna use this now as part of clearing negative energy and building energetic shields.

Clearing Negative Energy

The world is not always a happy place. Sometimes this means that you get swamped by negative energy. There are lots of ways to clear this, and I'm going to give you two to start out with.

When negative energy (whether it's someone else's energy or a DIY project) is bringing you down, one way to deal with it is an energy cleansing shower. Climb into the shower and park yourself under the water, letting it flow down on all sides of you. Close your eyes and picture that water as light. Set an intention that the light is flowing over you and through you, washing away any energy that is negative, unhealthy or not for your highest good. See that negative energy being washed away to the sea, where it is recycled into something positive and beneficial.

Pay attention to your body and what it tells you. When it relaxes and feels good again, you've cleared the negative energy and are ready to go about your day.

A second way of clearing negative energy is something that I call the 1 minute negative energy clear.

Start by rating how stressed you feel from 1-10, with 1 being "meh" and 10 being as bad as you can picture.

Then

- Take a deep breath.
- Keep your head level.
- Roll eyes up to look at the ceiling with head still level.
- Breathe out, and intend that the negative energy is being exhaled.

Now check your stress level number. Most people find they've dropped one level or more.

Rinse and repeat as many times as you like, until you get to 0 or at least to a level you can live with. Works like a charm.

One precaution: if you're slimed by negative energy because someone is giving you a hard time (a bad boss for instance), do not do this in front of them. If they're yelling at you and you roll your eyes, they're gonna yell even more. I find excusing myself and doing this release in a bathroom is helpful.

That's two ways to clear out negative energy. Try both of them and see which you prefer (or maybe you'll like both.)

Next, now that we've cleared the immediate negative energy, we'll talk about shielding yourself from further attacks.

Energetic Shielding

When you become more aware of the energy around you, sometimes it can be a lot to deal with. (It can be a lot to deal with even if you're not aware of it yet.)

Hostile work environment. Angry commuters. The malls at the holidays. It can be a lot to take and leave you feeling overwhelmed and irritable. And that's not even counting the times when people are personally angry with you.

At that point, you need energetic shields. Even before then, you need shields to keep other people's energy of any sort from mixing with your energy and swamping you.

But how do you get good energetic shields? You can't just go to the local department store and pick them up in the "energetic shields" department…

Let's start with a simple way to develop your energetic shields.

First, you should clear as much negative energy as you can, using a technique from the previous chapter or one of your own. You don't want to build a shield and shut the negative energy in with you.

Whenever you have a moment (or two, or ten…) close your eyes and picture yourself surrounded by light. Light on the left of you and the right; light in front of you and behind you; light over your head and under your feet; so that you're surrounded completely on all sides by light.

What color should the light be? Tradition holds that it should be white, as that is the highest/ purest/best color, and also contains all of the other colors within it.

I believe that you should chose whatever color makes you feel safest/calmest/ best with yourself.

- Like green? Great!
- Want pink? Right on!
- If you want plaid, I'm for it!

You can also have more than one color. My own shields tend to be white with a gold edge.

As you visualize the light, set an intention to define what you want your shields to do for you.

- Intend that you will be protected from any outside energy that could harm you in body, mind, or spirit.
- Intend that no other outside energy will directly touch yours unless you consciously decide to let it.
- Intend that you will be aware of the energy outside of your shields, but that it cannot affect you.
- Intend that your shields are always protecting you unless you consciously choose to let them down.

You get the idea.

What would you like your shields to do?

As you visualize your shields, you'll find over time that you feel more protected and more able to cope with the external energy that surrounds you. Once your basic shields are functioning, you can tweak your visualizations and/or your intent to fine-tune your shields to meet your unique needs.

Focus

Now that we've cleared out negative energy and created energetic shields to keep it out, let's talk about boosting your own energy levels higher. There's lots of ways to do this, and I'm going to teach you two to get started with.

We'll start with focus, which is both an important part of most methods of vibrational change and a technique for altering your energetic level on its' own. Focus is metaphysically working with energy. Amongst other things, it can be choosing a goal to send energy to or holding your attention on something in order to change your vibrational level.

We've already touched on focus briefly earlier in this booklet, but let's get more deeply into some ways to set and hold your focus.

To set and hold a focus, you can

- Hold an item or objective steadily in your mind.
- Play music that makes you feel the vibration you want. (Have theme music for specific tasks.)
- Fill your surroundings with items and pictures that remind you of your desired vibration or your goal.
- Post cards with words that describe what you're focusing on.
- Have a list of things (books, movies, activities, etc.) that uplift you.
- Have the things that uplift you easily available to you.
- Visualize what you're focusing on.
- Build a habit of naming your goals at least once per day.

- Write the things you're focusing on and post it where you'll see them frequently.
- Make a vision board.
- You can also use affirmations to change your beliefs, set your focus or improve your vibrational level- and we're going to talk about that next.

In short, you want to use whatever method (s) work best for you to bring your attention to what you're focusing on and keep it there as much as possible. You don't have to focus on your goals or on things that raise your energy nonstop, but the more you focus, the more you bring your energy to achieving what you're looking to do.

Affirmations

We all have beliefs, both conscious ones and unconscious ones, and those beliefs help to both shape our vibrational levels and the nature of reality around us. This can help us to have a good life or sabotage us, depending on what kind of beliefs we hold. The unconscious ones can be particularly tricky, setting the tune for our lives when we're not even aware what they are.

Our beliefs come from our programming. Things others have taught us. Things society has taught us. Things we've learned ourselves. And even if the sources of our beliefs meant well, not all of those beliefs are positive or will support us in being happy, healthy or successful. Every situation has multiple truths contained in it, and not all of those truths will take us in the direction we want to go.

So how can we change the negative beliefs? One way is affirmations.

Affirmations are positive statements, repeated to replace our negative beliefs. Negative beliefs come from negative lessons repeated until they stick in our spirits. Studies find that an affirmation, repeated 1000 times, will force the negative belief out and replace it. (My experience is that I start to see some results in less than 1000, but I always do the full number anyway.)

Affirmations are

- As short as possible. (ex: "I am healthy.")
- Stated in the present tense. (ex: "I am strong" as opposed to "I will be strong.")
- Stated in a positive way. (ex: "I am graceful." not "I am not clumsy.") For some reason, your unconscious

seems to edit out words like "no" or "not" (ex: hears "I am not exhausted" as "I am exhausted" and programs for that.)
- Easy to say/ not tongue twisters. (Try a potential affirmation out loud to see.)

Affirmations can be

- Repeated out loud.
- Repeated silently in your head.
- Written repeatedly on paper.
- Or repeated any other way that suits your fancy.

I find most of the affirmations I create take about 15 seconds or so to repeat 10 times. I like to repeat my affirmations in groups of 50 at a time, because it makes them pile up and start working faster without being tiring.

Affirmations are a great way to boost your vibrational level and improve your reality.

More Things to Learn

Well, we've taken a long trip in a short little booklet. You've learned about:

- Free will and how you can use it to choose a better life.
- How psychic readings interact with free will.
- Strengths and weaknesses of 6 types of psychic readings.
- The basics of energy work.
- About the Law of Attraction.
- And setting an intention.

You've also learned

- 2 different ways to tap into your psychic abilities.
- 2 ways to clear negative energy.
- 11 ways to focus energy.
- A simple way to create an energetic shield for yourself.
- How to create and use affirmations to clear negative beliefs and improve your reality.

Whew! That's all we have room for here, but there's a great big beautiful metaphysical universe out there if you decide you want to learn more.

To give you some ideas to start with:

- Interested in methods of psychic readings? Look at books or classes on tarot, palm, runes, oracle cards, the I Ching, pendulum dowsing or other modalities.

- Interested in alternative healing? Check out acupressure or Reiki.
- Interested in stilling your mind or changing beliefs? Look into meditation or do a search for Emotional Freedom Technique (E.F.T.)
- Into more active pursuits? Try Tai Chi, Qigong or walking meditations.

Just know that there's a lot of metaphysical wisdom out there just waiting for you if you so choose to look for it. This booklet is only the start.

Wishing you well on your journey.

Catherine Kane
Foresight

Your Notes

This book is dedicated to

Tchipakkan,
Beta reader and metaphysical reference extraordinaire!
Who came through for me not once but twice at the last minute!

And my husband, Starwolf,
Also an extraordinary metaphysical reference and authority, who plucked the words I needed out of my psyche to name this booklet, and who supports me as a writer in every possible way (bless him.)

It takes a village to raise a child. It takes a tribe to write a book.

Acknowledgements

Welcome to my twelfth book, the tenth book in general circulation. What a long strange trip it's been.

As always, my heartfelt thanks to Tchipakkan, who offered to beta read with extremely short notice, graciously accepted it when a cold and allergies made me back out at the last minute, who offered to beta read Again the following week when I crawled back to my keyboard, and came through a power outage to get me her feedback in the nick of time.

Wow. Greater love has no beta reader

My continuing gratitude to my readers and fellow writers who were kind and patient with me, encouraged me, gently nagged me, and kept me writing. What would I do without you?

Love and gratitude to the people and situations that made me the writer I am. I hope you're not sorry about that.

My thanks to the readers who've read my other books and have politely nudged me to get more of them out into the world. If you're new, welcome to my world.

And, as always, to my husband Starwolf, knowledgeable shaman, professional psychic, healer, multi-talented man of all works and general all round good guy. I write, but I couldn't do it without you, love.

Catherine Kane was raised by feral storytellers.

She's a teller of tales, a teacher, a poet, a wordsmith and a song wright, an artist, an enthusiastic student of the Universe, a maker of very bad puns and a medieval re-enactor who spends a fair amount of time at renaissance faires when she isn't hunched over her computer, writing.

She's also a bit of an over-achiever.

Want to know more about her?

Find her on Facebook at
https: / / www.facebook.com / Catherine-Kane-Writes / 134304556668759

www.ingramcontent.com/pod-product-compliance
Lightning Source LLC
Chambersburg PA
CBHW072017060426
42446CB00043B/2689